AVON SUPERSTARS

DAN MARINO
JOE MONTANA

by John Holmstrom

AVON SUPERSTARS

AVON BOOKS
A division of
The Hearst Corporation
1790 Broadway
New York, New York 10019

Copyright © 1985 by Avon Books
Published by arrangement with Parachute Press
ISBN: 0-380-75039-2

First Avon Special Printing, August 1985

AVON TRADEMARK REG. U. S. PAT. OFF. AND IN
OTHER COUNTRIES, MARCA REGISTRADA, HECHO EN
U. S. A.

Printed in the U. S. A.

OP   10   9   8   7   6   5   4   3   2   1

Front Cover Photos: Joe Montana from Fotosports
                     Dan Marino from Focus on Sports

Back Cover photos: Focus on Sports

Introduction

It seemed inevitable. Almost predestined. The two best football quarterbacks in the world, Dan Marino and Joe Montana, had to square off in the Super Bowl. Marino had set the football world on its ear in 1984, throwing more touchdown passes than anyone in NFL history, and establishing several other passing records along the way. Joe Montana led the San Francisco 49ers to an incredible 15-1 record, and came within a field goal of a perfect season!

But even before Super Bowl XIX, sportswriters and sports fans had noticed other similarities between Joe Montana and Dan Marino. To start with, they grew up within 25 miles of each other in western Pennsylvania. Both quarterbacks were undervalued in the NFL draft after suffering sub-par senior college seasons.

And throughout their careers, both quarterbacks seemed to have had great seasons in the same year. While Danny was in high school, dazzling college scouts, Joe was at Notre Dame, leading the Fighting Irish to some amazing last-minute wins. In 1980, Joe Montana won the starting quarterback job for the San Francisco 49ers. Dan Marino led his college team, the Pittsburgh Panthers, to a great 11-1 college season. In the 1981 season, Joe won the Super Bowl; Dan won the Sugar Bowl. 1982 was a year both would rather forget. In 1983 (Dan's first in the NFL), they both bounced back and their teams made the playoffs, but were bounced out in post-season play. And, in 1984, they met in the Super Bowl.

As similar as Montana and Marino are, there are also lots of differences. Their personalities are very different. Joe is quiet, soft-spoken, and shy. Dan, brash and flamboyant, has been described as the only man who struts while standing still.

It's the same on the field—they're as different as you could imagine. Mark Duper, Miami's super receiver, once described Marino's style of motivating his teammates to a reporter. "If he was somebody else, he might tick guys off, the way he is. He'll jump on your stuff right in the huddle." Once Marino got on Duper's case for missing one of his passes. "Run the thing right, Dupe," Marino screamed. "I'll run the pattern," Mark shouted back. "You just get me the ball!" Dan smiled, gave Mark five, and then connected with Mark for a first down. Montana takes the opposite approach. "The last thing a player wants to hear," he once commented, "is a teammate—a friend—yelling during a game."

When Joe and Dan met in Super Bowl XIX, the pre-game hype was incredible. It would be a Super Shootout. The perfect match-up. The

Super Bowl was going to be the greatest football game ever. No way it couldn't be. Until they played it. Then it turned into a Super Bore. It was all over by halftime.

The next time Joe Montana and Dan Marino faced each other on national TV, they appeared in a Diet Pepsi commercial. Joe asks, "Dan, can I buy you one?" To which Dan jokingly replies, "It's the least you can do!" Joe tosses a soda can to Dan, then says, "Here! Don't drop it." But Dan gets in the last word as they go their separate ways. "Joe! Next year, I'm buying."

It's possible. The San Francisco 49ers were the pride of the NFC in 1984. They lost one game. The Miami Dolphins lost only two games in the regular season, establishing themselves as the class of the AFC. Unless one team suffers disastrous injuries, or a dark-horse team gets lucky and puts it all together, there is a good chance they'll meet in Super Bowl XX. Then we'll see who buys the soda!

1

A Pittsburgh Guy

A few days before Super Bowl XIX got underway, a high school football coach dusted off some six-year-old black and white films of one of his former players. Rich Erdelyi, head football coach at Central Catholic High in Pittsburgh, wanted to see with his own eyes if Danny Marino was as good as he remembered. After viewing the films, he said, "He could do all these things before. Nothing Danny ever does surprises me."

In high school, Erdelyi ran a pro-style offense that allowed Dan to throw 400 times in his last two seasons. Sometimes youth and confidence cost him. In one game, Danny rolled left and tried to heave a throw across his body through three defenders. It was intercepted. "I remember telling him, 'The ball doesn't have eyes,' " the coach recalled. Dan answered, "You're pretty mad, huh?"

Danny's coach told him to just keep throwing. Two plays later, Danny hurled the ball 60 yards, a perfect pass. They won 19-18. In high school, Dan was such a threat that defenses played him soft, dropping way back. This allowed him to end up rushing for 600 yards.

Dan was taught by his dad to throw the ball with a short flick from the ear. "He wanted me to throw and not wind up," he said recently. "A lot of kids have the tendency to wind up and throw sidearm because they can throw it farther that way. But as I got stronger, I could throw it just as far."

And now Dan has the fastest release in the league, maybe the fastest release of all time. And it's that quick release that allows him to throw the ball before defenders can sack him.

Dan's father was a newspaper truck driver, and he worked nights. That left lots of time for him to play catch with Dan in the backyard. And Willie Stargell, the great Pittsburgh Pirates slugger, lived next door to Danny's grandmother. Dan used to play catch with Willie at Frazier Field and in the streets.

Pittsburgh is a key to understanding Dan Marino. He grew up in the tough Oakland district, five blocks from the University of Pittsburgh campus, and although he now lives near Miami, his heart is still in Pittsburgh. He still hangs around with the guys he went to school with, and brings them down to his place in Florida to stay with him. "As far as my friends go," he once said, "they're still the same. I'll always be around the neighborhood during the off-season. I don't forget where I came from.

I'm a Pittsburgh guy."

Danny went to St. Regis School, across Parkview Avenue, for eight years. He did very well at sports, but he didn't get good grades. A sixth-grade teacher once told his parents that their son would never graduate from high school. His mom cried. His father knew better. He figured that if his son could memorize everything he read on baseball cards, he could do well in school. By college, Danny was a B + student in communications.

After St. Regis, he went to Central Catholic High, four blocks from St. Regis. Rich Erdelyi says, "He always had his feet on the ground. He never was star-struck with himself."

The only trouble that he got in, besides a few noisy parties with his pals, was caused by an occasional lack of discipline. "He'd walk in," his father is fond of saying, "and leave the door open. I mean, how much athletic ability does it take to close the door?"

When anyone asks Danny Jr. who his hero is, or which coach had the greatest influence on him, he doesn't hesitate. He says it is his dad, because he was there every day after school to toss a football around, or hit a few hundred ground balls for him to field.

His father's strictest rule was that Danny was to play ball because he enjoyed it, not because his dad expected him to. And he impressed on

Danny Jr. that losing a game is not the end of the world, and that sports is the "reel" world, not the *real* world. He meant it was like the movies, not reality. His father would say, "Real pressure is having six kids, and half of them are sick, and you've been laid off at the mill. That's pressure. So if you lose, don't worry about it." Which helps explain why Dan is involved in a program that gives free shoes to children of unemployed workers for each touchdown pass he throws.

Danny's favorite quarterback as a kid was Terry Bradshaw, and not just because he was the quarterback of the Pittsburgh Steelers. "Bradshaw was tough," Dan told reporters before Super Bowl XIX. "He was a winner. He'd play hurt and do whatever it took."

Marino was highly recruited by college scouts after high school, and he toyed with the idea of going to UCLA or Clemson, but finally decided to stay close to home in Pittsburgh.

In Dan's room at home are jerseys worn by some of the great players who had played at Pitt—Tony Dorsett, Rich Trocano, Matt Cavanaugh—and trophies, plaques, and awards. What means the most to Danny are two pictures—one of his high school baseball team, the other of his high school football team. "Those are the real memories," he says.

2
Big Man on Campus

Dan Marino's college football career didn't start out easy at Pittsburgh. His first pass, thrown against Kansas, on September 15, 1979, was an interception. His second attempt almost was. But his third gave a hint of what was to come. It was a perfect pass that spiraled into the receiver's hands for a touchdown. As a freshman, he was second-string to Rich Trocano. But Rich, before long, decided to switch to safety. He knew he wouldn't see much more action at QB.

Dan's number, as always, was 13. He first wore it while he was playing for American Legion Post 663. When uniforms were handed out, the big sizes had numbers 13, 14, and 15, and two older players claimed 14 and 15. It was okay with Dan. "I'm not superstitious," he says.

He won the starting job after a few games, and was Pittsburgh's number-one quarterback. In his second year, after a few games, he suffered a knee injury, and was out for the rest of the year. Even though the injury wasn't serious, it kept him out of the lineup.

Just before his sophomore year, Dan Marino

had been offered a $50,000 signing bonus from the Kansas City Royals baseball team to play shortstop, but he turned it down. He figured a college education was worth more. As it turns out, he was more than right, even though he must have wondered if he made the right choice after he got injured.

Even when Dan was at college, his father was there for him. He used to send Dan notes that said things like, "Play relaxed and things will fall into place. On days when they don't, it's not the end of the world." The constant reassurance from his father helped Dan through his sometimes rocky four years at college.

At the start of Danny's junior year in 1981, things were looking good. He was nicknamed "Ice" because he was always so cool under pressure. He was Mister Touchdown. An All-America Hero. The answer to every NFL scout's dreams. He was going to be "the first quarterback drafted next year," without a doubt.

When Foge Fazio, Danny's coach, was asked about Marino's place on the team, he answered, "He IS the Pittsburgh football team. All he means to us is everything." Another former coach, Jackie Sherrill, said, "I played with Namath and Kenny Stabler at Alabama, and Marino is better than *any* of them at the same stage in their careers."

Danny was asked by a writer from *Sports Il-*

lustrated to sum up his own ability. He blurted out, "I throw better than anyone·in college. And I can throw with anybody in the pros. There, that's what I think. That sounds awful, doesn't it?" Dan has always tried not to sound cocky and overconfident, but he can't help it. A leopard can't change its spots, and Dan Marino can't stop being cocky.

Danny had good reason to strut in 1981. He led the Pitt Panthers to an 11-1 season, and was the top-rated college passer for most of the year. One of the highlights of the season was Dan's duel with Doug Flutie and Boston College. Pitt won 29-24, and Dan passed for two touchdowns and ran for another.

Pitt turned spoiler in the Sugar Bowl, beating Georgia, which had a shot at being named #1, 24-20. Georgia was led by the great running back, Herschel Walker. But Dan threw two touchdowns and was clearly the outstanding player of the game. It was billed as the opening round in the battle for next year's Heisman Trophy, which is given each year to the outstanding college player. Marino's team won the game, but it was Herschel who went on to win the Heisman.

The next year (1982), everyone thought Pittsburgh would be #1 all year. Dan Marino was expected to be outstanding, and most of the players from the defense would be back.

Things went wrong from the very beginning. The opening game, played on national TV, was against North Carolina. Although Pitt won, Dan threw four interceptions and was sacked five times. He seemed confused and unsure of himself. After the game, he wasn't considered a strong nomination for the Heisman Trophy anymore. And Pitt's #1 ranking was in doubt.

As the season wore on, Pitt was rated #1, but that was thanks to its defense, not to Danny Marino. He threw nine interceptions in the first three games. Pitt was winning despite Dan Marino, not because of him.

The bottom fell out in a game against Notre Dame. Before the smoke cleared, Notre Dame won, 31-16. And Dan had failed to throw a touchdown for the first time in 20 games.

Pitt's 9-3 record during his senior season was a big disappointment for Pitt fans who expected a national championship. But Dan's father thought that the "losing" season was the best thing for Danny Jr. He figured it taught Danny how to lose, and that losing a game won't kill you. Danny also learned how to get booed—Pitt fans gave him lots of practice at that.

After Dan's disappointing senior season, he had one more embarrassment to endure—the NFL draft. After coming in fourth in the voting for the Heisman Trophy, team after team passed on Dan. Five other quarterbacks were chosen before he was. Dan was shocked. He knew he'd had a disappointing season, but he also thought he was the best of the college quarterbacks.

Dan was finally chosen second to last in the first round, by the Miami Dolphins. That means that Danny was chosen after 26 other players had already been selected.

Things actually couldn't have worked out better for Dan. He was going to a team that had just played in the Super Bowl and he would be learning from one of the all-time great coaches, Don Shula.

Shortly after signing with the Dolphins for around two million dollars over four years, Danny bought a satellite dish for his father so his family could watch all the Dolphin games. He wanted to do even more for his family, but Dan Sr. wouldn't let him.

Dan dedicated himself to playing football. He even passed up a free trip to Italy in his first year because he didn't want to report late to the Dolphins' training camp. He figured he could always go to Italy some other time. This time was for football.

3
Miami's Superstar

Don Shula got Miami to the Super Bowl the year before Dan joined them despite the fact that their QB combo, David Woodley and Don Strock, had the league's worst quarterback rating. Experts did not expect much of the Dolphins in 1983.

In an exhibition game, they did manage to trounce the Washington Redskins 38-7. Dan threw a TD pass to contribute to the victory, but Woodley was the starter. Some writers, however, were a bit more impressed with Marino. "Dan Marino," one wrote, "has displayed both a strong and quick arm and a quick mind. Marino has been calling his own plays and might be ready to challenge Woodley as the number-one quarterback toward the end of the season."

But David Woodley also had a strong exhibition season, and he had the experience. So he won the starting job.

But the Miami offense had trouble getting on track early in the season. Coach Shula was not happy with the quarterbacking, so he was forced to take a look at his rookie. Dan saw his first regular-season action when he replaced Woodley in the second quarter against the New Orleans Saints, who won the game 17-7.

Danny next got into a game against the L.A. Raiders. Although he threw two late touchdown passes, Shula felt it was still too early to make any permanent changes in his offense.

Meanwhile, the team did their best to make Dan feel at home. "Don't worry," Lyle Blackwood, the great defensive back, would joke. "There's no pressure on you at all. There's just a whole team of Super Bowl veterans who aren't gonna be happy if you mess up!"

Dan finally won the starting quarterback job in the sixth game of the 1983 season against Buffalo. In the two previous losses, Marino had been the only QB to get Miami into the end zone—two TDs against the Raiders and one against the Saints.

In the Buffalo game, the Dolphins were behind 14-0 when Marino rallied them with a 268-yard, three-touchdown passing circus that put the Dolphins ahead 35-28, with three minutes to play. The Bills finally won in overtime, but after the game, Don Shula was smiling. Marino was taking charge!

Even the Bills were impressed with the Marvelous Marino. A Buffalo coach said, "Frankly, he did a lot more than I thought possible for a rookie. What a show!"

In the next game, the Dolphins rolled over the N.Y. Jets, 32-14. It was Dan's second start, and he threw for three touchdowns. Afterwards, he said, "I felt a little more confident this week."

The rest of the 1983 season was up and down for Marino and Miami. They beat Baltimore 21-7, but it was a mud-splattered contest and not the kind of game where a quarterback can shine. Marino was luckier against the L.A. Raiders—he opened the game with nine straight completions, passed for two TDs, and scored on a two-yard run. Miami won 30-14.

Next on the schedule was a big match-up with the 49ers—and Joe Montana. Although Dan completed 12 out of 17 passes for 145 yards in the first half, the promised passing duel never happened. Montana bruised a thigh in the third quarter, and the 49ers went to a running game. The Dolphins won 20-17.

Miami then lost to New England—in what Dan called his worst day as a pro. The next week he was back on track and threw an 85-yard TD bomb to Mark Duper. Miami shut out the Colts 37-0.

There would be other low points for Dan in his rookie season, and an injury to his knee made him miss two games. Still Dan's rookie season was almost as spectacular as the 85-yard touchdown pass against the Colts.

His record was truly incredible. He threw 20 touchdown passes, which missed the rookie record by only two, but he bettered Jim McMahon's rookie record for completion percentage (58.4 to 57.1). The biggest honor of all was that he became the first rookie quarterback to ever start in the Pro Bowl.

And maybe even more important than that honor was the praise that he received from coach Don Shula, who said that it was amazing that Danny got sacked only 10 times and threw only six interceptions in 306 pass plays. Coach Shula also pointed out that despite his inexperience, Danny was never indecisive, never seemed unsure of himself, no matter how much defenses tried to confuse him.

As great a year as Dan Marino and the Dolphins had in 1983, it ended too soon when the Seattle Seahawks beat them in their first playoff game. The season was over, but for Dan Marino, the best was yet to come.

4
The Natural

Dan Marino's 1984 season could go down as the greatest by any quarterback in NFL history.

A broken right index finger had limited his exhibition season to one appearance, so the world was unprepared for what happened next.

The very first regular-season game gave notice that Danny was about to perform the incredible. The Dolphins drubbed the Washington Redskins, who were just coming off their Super Bowl loss to the L.A. Raiders. The Dolphins' romp was due mostly to Dan Marino and Mark Duper. Dan was 21 of 28 for 311 yards and five TDs. Dan was not intercepted once, and completed 75 percent of his passes. He started the season with a 150.4 QB rating, and 158.3 is the highest possible score he could have had. Duper had six catches for 178 yards and two TDs.

Marino and Duper did it again the next week. Dan threw for 234 yards, and Mark caught six passes for 66 yards, and the Dolphins beat the New England Patriots 28-7. Dan did throw two interceptions, though, and he'd only done that once before in the pros.

The Dolphins went on a tear from there. Marino and Duper were the most dynamic passing combination in football history. Dan threw for 296 yards in the next game, and picked up three more touchdowns. He had 125 yards passing before Buffalo got a first down.

The Dolphins scored 44 points in their next game against the lowly Colts, then 36 against the St. Louis Cardinals. Dan suffered cramps in his throwing hand during the game. The trainers and doctors were trying to get salt in him to help stop the cramping. While he was being attended to on the sidelines, he looked down at his thumb and said, "Forget it. I'll just keep on throwing." He finished with a team-record 429 yards and three touchdowns, breaking the Dolphin single-game yardage record of 408.

Marino, at 6'3" and 214 pounds, doesn't run well, but he avoids the rush very well. At this point in the season, he'd been sacked only twice. And his four TD passes gave him 24 for the year, two more than Bob Griese's club record—and the season was only half over.

No other quarterback in history terrorized defenses so early in their careers, not Bradshaw, not Namath, not Bart Starr. "I never expected this kind of season," Dan admitted. "It helps to be playing on a great team. How we do depends on who blocked, who ran, who caught the pass. Not just how I passed. I'm not saying I'm the best quarterback in the league. That's up to others to decide."

But teams were getting geared up to play the Dolphins. They wanted to be the team to end the Dolphins' undefeated season. That honor went to San Diego, but they had to do it by beating the Dolphins in overtime, 34-28.

The Dolphins got back on track the next week and eliminated the N.Y. Jets' faint playoff hopes as Dan's four touchdown passes tied him with Y. A. Tittle and George Blanda as the only players to throw 36 TD passes in a season. Marino was three months old when Blanda set the record with the 1961 Oilers, and he was just a little kid when Tittle did it with the 1963 New York Giants.

The L.A. Raiders ruined Marino's day when they beat the Dolphins 45-34. The Raiders threw every kind of defense against Marino that they could—especially blitzes of every size, shape, number, and form. The game lasted 14 minutes short of four hours. Marino had a personal-best game—470 yards passing and four touchdowns, which gave him 40 for the season, and broke the record. But football is a team sport and since the team lost, Dan's day was ruined.

The last game of the season was an incredible *Monday Night Football* finish to an amazing season. The Dolphins beat the Dallas Cowboys 28-21 in front of one of the largest TV audiences ever to see a Monday-night game. Nonstop fourth-quarter fireworks saw Mark Clayton finish the game with three touchdown catches to give him 18, the most in NFL history. The last catch was the game-winner, and Dan's 48th of the season. It gave him 5,084 passing yards for the season, breaking the old record set by Dan Fouts. Dallas was out of the playoffs for the first time since 1974.

In the first post-season game, Miami got revenge for last year and rolled over the Seattle Seahawks, 31-10.

Then they faced the Pittsburgh Steelers—and Dan did not treat his old hometown heroes kindly. He shredded the defense for 421 yards passing and set a new record for TDs in a title game with four. Dolphins 45, Steelers 28.

Dan Marino's spectacular season had led Miami to the AFC championship. But now he had one more challenge to face—Super Bowl XIX against the San Francisco 49ers—and their great quarterback, Joe Montana.

5
Joe College

Joe Montana started playing football when he was eight years old, in Monongahela, Pennsylvania. Once he told his dad that he didn't feel like being on the team anymore. His father told him no way and wouldn't let him quit. He had spent a lot of time getting Joe interested in sports, and he wasn't going to let his kid ruin everything for himself just because he felt like quitting one day.

His father told him to get his equipment and practice! He also told Joe that, one day, "things are going to get tough in your life, and you're going to want to quit. I don't believe in that."

That message must have sunk in, since Joe Montana hasn't quit yet, as any of his teammates can tell you. Throughout his history as a quarterback, Joe has brought his team back when things looked impossible.

Joe was lucky to have a father who let him practice. In fact, he wouldn't let Joe get a job in high school. Joe's father, who was the manager of a finance company (and his mother worked as the secretary there), figured that "working is for adults," and wouldn't let Joe waste valuable practice time pumping gas or scooping ice cream.

It paid off. Joe was a star in high school football, baseball, and basketball. He also competed in track, until it got in the way of baseball. He could, and did, play nine positions in baseball. Some people thought Joe should have been a pitcher. After all, in Little League he had pitched more than one perfect game! His father thought he was a natural infielder. Others thought he belonged in the outfield, since his batting average was around .500. In basketball, he played center, forward, and guard—sometimes in the same game!

But his heart was set on tossing that oblong apple—the football. By his senior year at Ringgold High School, Joe was heavily recruited by dozens of top football colleges. But Joe was set on Notre Dame, the most famous football university in America.

Joe's freshman and sophomore years at Notre Dame were no indication of what was to come later in his college career. Although he got into a few games, and sometimes performed well, he spent most of those two years on the bench, waiting his turn. In the Notre Dame football program, underclass quarterbacks are expected to spend those years learning.

In Joe's junior year, in 1977, Dan Devine, the head coach, chose Rick Slager as his starting quarterback at the beginning of the season. Joe was still on the bench. Notre Dame beat Pittsburgh in the first week, 19-9, but Devine was not happy with his offense. And when the Irish lost to Mississippi, 20-13, writers called the Notre Dame offense a "Laurel and Hardy production." They were that laughable. Devine was under enormous pressure from impatient fans and the media.

So, the next week, Joe Montana made his first appearance, and he did it in spectacular fashion. Montana took charge of the team in the fourth quarter. The team was down 24-14, but Joe ignited a 17-point explosion to win 31-24, completing nine passes for 154 yards. One set up a field goal, one was a touchdown, and one set up the winning touchdown.

At that point, Devine started hearing it in the press for not starting Montana. "All that Montana had done for Notre Dame," pointed out one writer, "is win games." Devine was on the hot seat, so he started Montana in the next game.

Notre Dame, with Joe behind the wheel, caught fire. Notre Dame's passing attack was finally noticed by the media, who said it was the most sophisticated in college football.

Notre Dame got an invitation to the Cotton Bowl. There they faced a great unbeaten Texas team, led by superb running back Earl Campbell. Joe Montana (99 completions for 1,064 yards and 11 TDs in only nine games) was Notre Dame's big gun.

Notre Dame beat Texas 38-10, and won the national championship. Notre Dame played a perfect game, but most of the attention went to the defense. Joe was almost perfect himself. But in spite of the fact that all he did was win games, he wasn't a hero. Not yet.

Joe picked up the nicknames "the Comeback Kid" and "Miracle Man" for the thrilling, come-from-behind victories he engineered as a junior. Before his senior year, he was a likely choice for the Heisman Trophy.

Then Notre Dame lost its first game, 3-0, to the Missouri Tigers. Missouri stopped Notre Dame on several crucial fourth-down situations, and intercepted two of Joe's passes—not exactly a Heisman Trophy-winning performance from Mr. Montana.

The second game of the season was even worse. Notre Dame was winning at halftime, 14-7, but lost the game 21-14. The lowlight of the game came in the last minute—Joe was sacked in the end zone for a safety. Joe threw for a touchdown, but also threw two interceptions. The Notre Dame offense was hardly blowing opponents off the field. Joe's hopes for the Heisman Trophy were down the drain.

Joe shook off his "sleeping sickness" after that. He started passing well and led his team to victories over Michigan State and Pittsburgh. Dan Marino was still in high school when Notre Dame played Pittsburgh, so a college match-up between Montana and Marino never happened. Instead, Joe outdueled Pitt quarterback Rich Trocano. Notre Dame was down 17-7 when Joe got hot in the fourth quarter. He completed seven straight passes for 109 yards and two touchdowns, and scored the winning TD on a one-yard sneak.

Finally, Joe Montana and Co. were playing as they were supposed to. And just in time. Their next game was against the top defense in college football, unbeaten Navy. The game, played in Cleveland's Municipal Stadium in front of 63,780 people and millions more on TV, wasn't even close. Notre Dame torpedoed Navy 27-17, rolling up 530 yards in total offense. Notre Dame's outstanding running back, Vagas Ferguson, did most of the damage and got most of the attention with 218 rushing yards.

Joe's last college game was the Cotton Bowl against the Houston Cougars. He said at the time, "We're going back to the place where we won a national championship. The memories are there and we have a chance to play a good football team and redeem ourselves after our poor start." Joe was on a roll—after throwing six interceptions in the first two games, he threw only three after that, and rushed for six touchdowns. He established himself as one of the best college quarterbacks of 1978.

Only 10,000 people stayed throughout the freezing cold temperatures to watch the greatest Cotton Bowl comeback ever. The temperature on the field dropped below 22 and the wind was blowing at 30 miles an hour to create a wind-chill factor of six below zero.

Notre Dame had jumped out 12-0 in the first half and Joe scored the first touchdown. But he was feeling sick, and had to leave the game. "I wasn't sick," Joe said later, "I was just cold. My body temperature was below normal." In fact, his body temperature dropped to 96. The team doctors and trainers wrapped him in blankets and coats and fed him soup to get his body temperature back to normal.

Houston rallied, and Joe went back in the game in the middle of the third quarter. Houston was totally in control, ahead 34-12, with only 7:37 left in the game. It was then that Montana took over. With great running and the help of a super defense, he led Notre Dame to within a touchdown. At 2:05 left, he faded back to pass, then scrambled to the Houston 20. On the next play, he fumbled when a Houston linebacker hit him. Montana returned to the sidelines and told a teammate, "It's all over." There wasn't going to be a miracle.

But the Irish got another chance when

Houston was forced to punt. When Notre Dame was offside on the punt, the Houston coach decided to go for it on a fourth and sixth situation. Notre Dame stopped the attempt cold. They had the ball, but they still had 29 yards to go for the tying touchdown. A PAT would win the game. But time was running out!

Montana ran for 11 yards, then threw a 10-yard pass. Six seconds left. Notre Dame needed eight yards. Montana threw a pass into the end zone. Incomplete. Two seconds left. He called the same play—and this time it worked! Tie score, 34-34.

With no time left on the clock, Notre Dame went for the extra point, but there was a penalty on the play. It was very tense in the stadium. The center snapped the ball. The holder placed it down and the kicker aced it through the uprights.

The Comeback Kid had done it again! One of the all-time great comebacks in the history of college football was over.

So was Joe Montana's college career. But an amazing pro career was about to begin.

6
Joe the Pro

On January 9th, 1979, just days after the thrilling Cotton Bowl comeback, Bill Walsh was named coach of the San Francisco 49ers. Bill Walsh was famous for complicated pass offenses, *and* his ability to bring out the best in quarterbacks. He coached Ken Anderson of Cincinnati, Dan Fouts at San Diego, and Steve Dils at Stanford University. Bill had been an assistant coach in the NFL for ten years, and had coached Stanford University for two.

One of the most difficult things to accomplish in sports is to turn around a team that's been losing for a long time. And the 49ers were a terrible team. Coach Walsh went to work right away. The 49ers had traded away their first-round draft choice, so he drafted James Owens, a running back they thought they could turn into a wide receiver, in the second round. Then he chose Joe Montana in the third round. (He also picked up wide receiver Dwight Clark in the tenth round.) Three quarterbacks went before Joe in the first round.

It was a lucky accident that Walsh ended up with Joe Montana. Joe's bad start the year before had led to doubts about him. Some of the scouts said he didn't have it.

There's an old saying in sports: "I'd rather be lucky than good." Joe is both. The first stroke of luck came when he met John Brodie, a former 49er quarterback and now a football commentator for NBC-TV. They were at a Hall of Fame dinner in New York shortly after Joe's senior season. Brodie was very impressed with Joe. "Quarterbacks are funny," Brodie said later. "You can usually tell as much about them from talking with them as any other way. I just saw an awareness, the way he handled himself. The next time I saw Bill Walsh, I told him if I had my choice I'd draft that Montana guy."

Then came a second stroke of luck. When Bill invited James Owens to a workout, he asked him to bring along someone who could throw the ball, so they could see him catch some passes. Montana happened to be in Los Angeles at the time working out with the Rams, so Owens called him.

"I'll admit I went along hoping to impress Coach Walsh," Montana said. "I knew the 49ers were looking for a quarterback. I figured, 'Well, if I have a good day, it can't hurt.' I did throw the ball well, and I got to talk to Coach Walsh. As he was leaving, he said, 'Keep in shape, Joe. You might be hearing from us on draft day.'"

Joe told *People* magazine how he felt about

being picked so late in the draft. "That didn't bother me. I know some first- and second-round choices who never made it. I had confidence in myself."

Although Coach Walsh has a lot of good things to say about Joe as a quarterback today, it wasn't exactly love at first sight. The main reason Joe was drafted was that both 49er quarterbacks at the time had knee problems. The 49ers needed insurance.

According to NFL wisdom, it takes a rookie quarterback three years to adjust to the pros, so Joe was expected to sit on the bench. He sat while the 49ers lost their first two games. But since the 49ers were doing so poorly, Coach Walsh decided to give him a try.

His pro debut had a dramatic setting, but it was no masterpiece. The 49ers were playing the Rams in Anaheim, California. It was 100 degrees, and there were roaring brush fires in the hills behind the stadium. Joe threw one pass for eight yards.

He went back to the bench as the 49ers lost their fourth, fifth, sixth, and seventh games.

The 49ers finally won against the Atlanta Falcons, and Joe got to play. He threw a pass, but the play lost eight yards. Joe watched the 49ers lose the next three in a row from the bench.

The 49ers lost again the next week, but at

It's Dapper Dan—doing what he does best—passing the football.
Fotosport

Dan Marino and his college team, The Pittsburgh Panthers. The score of this one against Rutgers College—52-6!
AP/Wide World Photos

No wonder he feels like number one!
AP/Wide World Photos

As a pro in Miami, continuing his winning ways!
Fotosport

Sometimes you've got to do it yourself . . . Marino scrambles.
AP/Wide World Photos

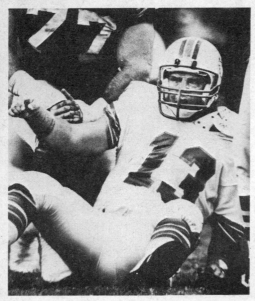

Sometimes you get help . . . Dan watches as Jimmy Cefalo catches Marino's thirty-seventh pass to break the NFL season TD passing record.
AP/Wide World Photos

Dan receives . . .
the Pro Football Writers Award in 1984
UPI/Bettmann Newsphotos

Dan gives . . .
free sneakers were
given to needy
kids for every TD
Marino scored in
1984.
AP/Wide World Photos

Mom and Dad—Veronica and Dan Marino, Sr.

And they lived happily ever after . . .
Dan married Claire Veazy in the church he attended as a boy.

Joe Montana back to pass!
Fotosport

Joe calls the signals.
Fotosport

Joe College goes to Japan.
Notre Dame's Joe Montana played in the Japan Bowl American
Collegiate All-Star football game. Here he signs an autograph
for one fan.
AP/Wide World Photos.

On the sidelines—Super Bowl XIX—no wonder he's smiling!
AP/Wide World Photos

Watch out, Joe! That's Lawrence Taylor behind you!

Montana runs 53 (!) yards against the New York Giants.

He's her MVP, for sure.
Joe's mother, Theresa Montana, congratulates her son.
UPI/Bettmann Newsphotos

Sport magazine has a different way of showing appreciation — The Super Bowl MVP Trophy.
UPI/Bettmann Newsphotos

SUPER BOWL XIX
The Thrill of Victory . . .
UPI/Bettmann Newsphotos

The Agony of Defeat . . .

But Dan's got his eye on the future . . .
Fotosports

least Joe threw his first NFL touchdown pass. The 49ers lost the next week, too.

Coach Walsh figured he had nothing to lose. He let Montana start at quarterback the week after, the 49ers' 14th game. Joe didn't perform well, completing five passes out of 12 attempts for only 36 yards. The 49ers scored only a field goal in the first half, and they lost to the St. Louis Cardinals, 13-10.

The 49ers beat the Tampa Bay Buccaneers the next week, and Joe did contribute to the win, completing three passes for 30 yards. But no one could say he had set the world on fire in 1979.

It was a tough adjustment for Joe—a real jolt to go from a college team that had won a national title to the bench of a team that went 2-14. But Joe hung in. He figured things had to get better in 1980, right?

7

Joe Starts

Wrong.

Walsh was satisfied with his quarterback tandem. In 1980, he decided Steve DeBerg would start, and Joe Montana would be the backup. It looked as if Joe Montana was going to sit on the bench for the rest of his career.

But opportunity knocks more than once when you play for a loser. And the 49ers were losers. Joe got his ticket to leave the bench after Dallas stomped the 49ers 59-14!

Walsh felt that DeBerg couldn't avoid the rush as well as Joe, and he threw interceptions at the worst times. Joe had his problems, too—he wasn't picking up blitzes quickly enough. A blitz is when the defense sends linebackers or safeties right into the offensive backfield to try and help sack the quarterback.

So Joe and Steve still shared the quarterback duties. Joe wasn't playing well enough to win the job outright. Reports in the papers said that Walsh had given up on DeBerg, and the 49ers were going to trade for a quarterback. They said Walsh was putting Joe into games to give him some practice so he'd be ready to play as their backup quarterback.

The turning point came for Joe against the New England Patriots. The pass defense of the Patriots was one of the best. The 49ers didn't have a chance, according to football experts.

But the Niners beat the Pats 21-17. Joe threw three touchdowns. This game meant a lot to San Francisco. They beat a very good team, and Montana performed well. They won the next game, too, beating the New Orleans Saints.

The Niners finished the season 6-10. Not great, but Joe had convinced his coach and his team that he could do the job. The San Francisco 49ers could concentrate on rebuilding the rest of the team. They had their quarterback.

Steve DeBerg was Joe's friend and roommate. "It was tough," Joe told *People*. Joe won the quarterback slot, but lost his friend in the deal—Steve was traded away. "Steve and I roomed together on the road, and after we checked into a hotel we'd head right down to the game room. We'd try to beat each other at anything. Being a quarterback means you want to be on top," he said.

The 49ers were on their way. But no one, not even the 49ers, realized that, after a 6-10 season, just what they would pull off the next year.

Let's be honest. Nobody in his right mind thought the San Francisco 49ers even had a chance of making the playoffs in 1981. Especially after their first game. In a pitiful performance, they lost 24-17 to Detroit. Ironically, the game was played at the Silverdome, Detroit's home field. No one suspected they'd be back there to play the Super Bowl.

The 49ers beat the Chicago Bears 28-17 in their next game, but then lost to the Atlanta Falcons, 34-17. The game's big play came when Joe threw an interception that was returned 101 yards for a clinching touchdown.

The team was looking for respectability, and so was Joe. He got it the old-fashioned way— he earned it. Against the Dallas Cowboys.

On October 11th, the 49ers faced the mighty Cowboys, the same team that had dealt them their most embarrassing defeat the year before. And Joe Montana had his best day as a pro. He completed 18 passes for 279 yards and two touchdowns. And he wasn't intercepted once. The 49ers won the game 45-14. It was the Dallas Cowboys' biggest loss since 1970. Coach Walsh said after the game, "We're maturing, but it will take another draft or two before we are a Super Bowl team."

But something happened to make them mad enough to get them there two years early. The biggest win in San Francisco history wasn't shown on ABC's *Monday Night Football* halftime highlights. In fact, the 49ers hadn't appeared on *Monday Night* highlights all year. The team blasted ABC for the oversight. But the incident gave the 49ers a real motive. Now they wanted more than respectability. And now, they were *mad*.

The next week, the 49ers beat the Green Bay Packers 13-3. It was their fourth straight win, and they took over first place in their division. Then they beat the Rams for the first time in 10 games.

Their next game was in Pittsburgh. Very few teams beat the Pittsburgh Steelers at Three Rivers Stadium in the 1970s. But the 49ers won 17-14, even though Joe was picked off twice in the third quarter.

It wasn't until the 49ers seventh win in a row that Joe started getting some recognition. He was the leading passer in the NFC. Reporters started asking Joe Walsh why Joe was such a great quarterback. Walsh said, "He always knows where everybody is, or should be, on a given play. He has fantastic downfield vision and instinct. That is the difference between being a mechanical man and a potentially great quarterback. So far, he has done some things we didn't expect to happen until next year or maybe even 1983."

The 49ers beat the Rams again, then wrapped up the division title by beating the N.Y. Giants. And they did it by riding Joe's arm.

In fact, they rode Joe's arm all the way to the championship game against—guess who?—Dallas.

The 49ers beat Dallas 28-27. The play of the game was a six-yard touchdown pass to Joe's favorite receiver, All-Pro Dwight Clark. The victory avenged three 49er playoff losses to Dallas in 1970, '71, and '72. The next stop was the Super Bowl against the Cincinnati Bengals.

In the 18 games leading to the Super Bowl, Joe's passing averaged 231 yards a game. In the Super Bowl he totaled 157 yards on 14 completions in 22 attempts. The Bengals' QB, Ken Anderson, a former student of Walsh's, threw 25 for 34 for 300 yards. But Joe won the MVP award, as the 49ers won, 26-21. Never before had a team improved so fast—from 2-14 to 13-3 in the regular season and a Super Bowl victory in only two years.

After the game, Joe said that winning the Supe was necessary to get football people to take the 49ers seriously. "We won some big games, but people around the country just didn't believe we had a good team. Even after we beat Dallas the second time [in the title game], people just didn't seem to believe in us."

He also admitted that the Super Bowl wasn't on the 49ers' minds at the beginning of the year. "It was tough to think Super Bowl early. We were just thinking about improving our record, compared to what we had done the past two years."

Montana tied Namath as the youngest quarterback to win a Super Bowl. Joe Montana was born on June 11, 1956, and played the game January 24, 1982, 25 years and 227 days later. Joe Namath was born May 31, 1943, and played January 12, 1969, 25 years and 226 days later. But there were seven leap years between Namath's birth and his Super Bowl and only six for Montana, so they tied. At least that's what it says in the record book.

After the Super victory, Joe went to Hawaii to play in the Pro Bowl, then went on an African safari to shoot animals—with a camera. If he knew what 1982 would be like, he probably would have stayed there.

8
Just Plain Joe

After their spectacular Super Bowl victory, the 49ers had to battle the Super Bowl "curse." Teams that win the Super Bowl have a bad habit of going backwards the next year. Other teams get more pumped up when they play against the champs. After a team wins it all, there's a lot of pressure in the off-season—appearances, publicity, etc. Petty jealousies between players can develop. Some players get lazy. They forget what it takes to win.

Walsh did his best to avoid the trap, but the 49ers fell into it anyway. Everything that could go wrong for them did. The team was devastated by freak accidents and personal problems that affected their offensive line, and the 49ers struggled.

They lost their first two games. Then things really got bad. The team didn't win another game for seven weeks. They didn't lose any games, either, because they didn't play any games for seven weeks. The football strike began after two weeks of the 1982 season, just after the Monday-night game between the Packers and the Giants. It was the first work stoppage in the 63-year history of the NFL.

When the strike did finally end, seven weeks were lost. At 0-2, the 49ers knew they would have to put it together fast if they wanted to make the playoffs.

In the first game after the strike, the 49ers beat the Cardinals, 31-20, and Joe established a club record and set a personal high of 408 yards, on 26 completed passes. He credited the practice he and the receivers put in during the strike. "We started out five days a week for the first two or three weeks," he admits, "but then it dropped off. We still tried to play three or four times a week."

Maybe they should have practiced more often. The 49ers finished up the 1982 season 3-6. After reaching the top in 1981, the 49ers hit the bottom in 1982. Coach Walsh was critical of the team and the way they played. He hinted that there would be drastic changes in the off-season.

Joe Montana was doing his best. But was it enough? Then, after the season ended, it came out that Joe's elbow on his throwing arm was hurt so badly that he took cortisone shots and underwent acupuncture treatments to stop the pain.

It also hadn't been easy for Joe to adjust to the changes in his life. He had gone from a backup quarterback for a last-place team to

Super Bowl Joe—all in just two years. Other men might welcome the sudden fame, the chance to see their faces all over magazine covers. But not Joe.

"I'm just plain Joe," he said of himself to a sports magazine. "People think, 'He's a star quarterback. He should do things this way or that way.' But I do things the same way you do. I eat the same way you do. I drive the same way you do, I use self-service gas stations, I wash my own car."

Joe tries to keep his private life private, but it's difficult—everybody wants his time, his money, a piece of him. "It's a trap, and the more you win, the worse it gets. For instance, the other night we went to the movies, and even though we were sitting in the balcony, people were coming up in the dark to get autographs. Nothing's private. I'm not bitter—it's part of the whole package. But it gets out of control sometimes."

He and his wife, Jennifer, the beautiful woman who plays the sheriff in Joe's commercial for disposable razors, plan to buy a house on the beach in Southern California, where he hopes to disappear among other celebrities and try to lead a more nomal life. "I love San Francisco and the Bay Area, but it's just too hectic to try to do day-to-day things."

Of course success does have its rewards. Joe's

new six-year contract will pay him 6.9 million dollars! "If I sit back and think about it, then it does boggle the mind," says just plain Joe.

The 1983 season started off badly too. In their opening 22-17 loss to the Philadelphia Eagles, the apparent winning touchdown was nullified by a holding penalty, with only 11 seconds left. Joe had to leave the game three times. The second time, he was trying to make a tackle after one of his passes was intercepted. The first game set the tone—Joe was in for a rough year.

The 49ers started winning, though. They beat the Vikings, then the Cardinals, the Falcons, the Patriots, the Saints, and the Rams in convincing fashion. The offense was playing better than ever, prompting Joe to remark, "We're playing more as a unit offensively than we did in our Super Bowl season." Coach Walsh remarked after one of the victories, "I'm almost in awe of these guys when they play like this."

Then the trouble started again. The N.Y. Jets, whom the 49ers had humiliated so long ago, beat San Francisco 27-13. The Niner rushing attack was so weak, Joe was the leading rusher with 50 yards. The Jets were able to put pressure on Joe. The killer was a Montana pass intercepted with 57 seconds left that was run in for a TD.

The most disturbing trend was that the loss was the seventh home loss out of the last eight games for the 49ers. Except for the victory against the Rams, they were playing terribly at home.

So Coach Walsh took his team to the 'Stick (Candlestick Park) before they faced the Miami Dolphins. The 49ers, like everybody who plays at Candlestick, were having trouble with the wind, so Walsh had them practice there on Saturdays before home games.

It didn't work right away. The Dolphins beat the 49ers, 20-17. But the 49ers won two games in a row after that, and were on the way to the playoffs again.

Dwight Clark was still Joe's favorite receiver. "In the back of my mind I look for Dwight when something goes wrong," Joe said after a win. "But that is only because I have confidence in him. I know that when I react, he is going to react. When I'm in trouble, I know that he is going to find a hole somewhere. I've never been one to sit back in the pocket and wait and wait and wait. Sometimes it works against me because I didn't look for the third or fourth guy."

Coach Walsh saw it this way, "Joe seems to be at his best in situations that are most difficult."

The 49ers won the division title, and faced

the Detroit Lions and won 24-23. The 49ers felt they had finally beaten their problems at home, since the game was played at the 'Stick. Next, they faced the Washington Redskins, who had won the Super Bowl the year before.

Joe was "the Comeback Kid" again in the game against the Redskins, but the 49ers came up short, losing 24-21. The Redskins led 21-0 after three quarters. But Joe led the 49ers to three touchdowns, and the score was tied. But the Redskins managed a field goal to seal their victory. Joe completed 27 of 48 passes for 347 yards, but his last attempt was intercepted to end the game. The '83 season was ended too.

9
Super!

The 49ers felt they had something to prove in 1984. They thought they should have been in the Super Bowl the year before. So they set out to do it again.

They won the home opener against the Lions 30-27. Next up were the Redskins. The 49ers owed them one. They paid it back in full, winning 37-31.

Coach Walsh down-played the revenge factor after the game, but the Niners had played ferociously. The game was played on a Monday night, so the national audience watched as their explosive offense got a 27-0 lead after 27 minutes. Joe passed for 211 of his 331 yards in the first half, moving the 49ers to three touchdowns and a pair of field goals.

The 49ers won the next week, but Montana was hurt and Matt Cavanaugh took his place in the third quarter. Joe had bruised ribs and a bruised sternum. He missed the next game, and when he did come back in the following game, he had to wear a padded flak jacket to protect his ribs. Joe was hurting, but his game was fine.

In fact, the Niners lost only one game all season—to the Steelers. And it was close. Kicker Ray Wersching missed a 37-yard field goal attempt, set up by Joe Montana on a series of passes, that would have tied the game with seven seconds left. The Steelers' winning field goal was set up by Joe's second interception of the year with 1:43 left in the game.

Joe finished the year as the NFC's top-rated passer, with a career-high 28 touchdown passes. Only Dan Marino kept him from the best rating in the NFL.

All of the media hype revolved around Dan Marino and his fearsome attack on the TD pass record; or on the Dolphins' bid to become the first team to go through the season undefeated; or on Mark Clayton's record for touchdown passes.

While the 49ers rolled to the most wins in the history of the NFL, they did it on defense—and defense doesn't make headlines. But it does win football games, as Dan Marino and company were to learn.

10
The Super Showdown

There had never been a Super Bowl show-down between the game's highest rated passers before. In fact, Joe Montana was the NFL's highest rated passer of all time. Marino actually rated higher, but didn't have enough pass attempts to qualify for the official record.

Most of the pre-game hype was about Dan Marino. It was as if Super Bowl XIX was his personal showcase. Everyone else was just there to watch.

As usual, Joe Montana and his 49ers were buried in the small print. The newspapers couldn't have given Joe a better motive for turning in the game of his life if they'd tried.

The 49er defense was even more fired up. They sat back and licked their lips as they read all the "ink" Marino got. Once they stopped Disco Dan Marino, they'd get all that ink. They'd been there before. They knew. The bigger they are, the harder they fall!

At game time—even with all the Marino press—the 49ers were favored to win by about three points. Since they were playing at nearby Stanford Stadium, this was like a home game for them. And their fans would be in the stands to cheer them on.

Were they ever! Ticket prices for Super Bowl XIX hit an all-time high. Some people actually paid $1,500 for a ticket. People were offering everything from video-tape recorders to hot tubs for tickets.

Before the game, the 49ers were careful to say all the right things. The San Francisco defensive coaches told the media how the team was impressed with Marino's performances on the game films. Secondary coach Ray Rhodes said about Marino: "Isn't this guy phenomenal?" And defensive coordinator George Seifert told *Newsweek*, "We all realize that there really is no way to stop this guy completely." But, of course, all week the 49ers prepared to do just that!

The Dolphins enjoyed all the praise the media were heaping on Marino. "We captains could give Danny a game ball for every game," Miami defensive back Glenn Blackwood said, playing a game of "Can You Top This?" with reporters at the Super Bowl press conferences. "People keep asking me for new ways to describe him, and I just say, 'He's for real. There's nothing bogus about him.' He's always the first to say 'I'm not great. We're great.' Outside of that, I can't stand the guy."

Right before the game, the pressure seemed

to be getting to the Dolphins. Marino was criticized for cutting some interviews short. He complained of wooziness after taking some medicine for an upset stomach. Mark Clayton popped off a few days before the game and bragged that San Francisco's secondary would not hold him.

For dyed-in-the-wool football fans, the wait was unbearable. The last few Super Bowls had been totally boring. The Miami-San Francisco match-up looked like a Super Bowl that would finally live up to its hype.

Before it turned into a massacre, the game *was* really exciting. The Dolphins got the ball, drove down the field, and, after seven plays, got three points on a field goal. San Francisco answered back right away by scoring a touchdown. Eight plays ate up 78 yards. The drive was topped off by a 33-yard pass play to seldom-used running back Carl Monroe.

The Dolphins came right back. They scored a TD in six plays. Marino looked as if he was going to do it. At the end of the first quarter, he was 8 for 10 for 103 yards, and one touchdown.

But the Miami offense fell apart! The Dolphins could manage only one yard in their next three possessions. Dan Marino went one for six for four yards. The 49ers stopped the Dolphin running game dead—they *lost* three yards in the second quarter.

While Miami was struggling, Montana put the game in his back pocket, helped by three poor punts by Joe Robie. He led the 49ers from three points down to 18 points up in the second quarter. The first TD, an eight-yard Joe Montana toss to Roger Craig, took only four plays.

Another poor punt left the Niners at their own 45 with 9:41 left, and they needed only six plays to score. Joe saw that his intended receiver, Clark, was covered, so he scrambled six yards into the end zone himself. The 49ers had all the points they needed.

The next touchdown really sealed the Dolphins' fate. The 49ers drove 52 yards in nine plays, making the score 28-10. The drive was helped along when a referee made an obvious bad call, a terrible call. Niner wide receiver Freddie Solomon caught a pass, then fumbled it when Lyle Blackwood hammered him. The play was called an incompletion instead of a fumble. If the Dolphins could have scored on the turnover, the score would have been 21-17, and the 49ers' confidence might have been shaken. Instead, the Niners capitalized on it. They picked up a first down on the next play, and scored a TD four plays later when Roger Craig ran two yards into the end zone.

The Dolphins scored two quick field goals

moments before the half ended, thanks to some sloppy play by the Niners, but it wasn't enough. The first half was over, and, as it turned out, so was the game. The Niner defense shut down the Dolphin offense the rest of the way. San Francisco scored a field goal and another touchdown to make it 38-10, then ran the ball, even on a fourth down, to keep from embarrassing the Dolphins any more.

Marino was sacked four times, and ended the day 29 for 50, for 318 yards with one touchdown and two interceptions. It was only the second time in his career that he'd thrown more interceptions than touchdowns. He'd been sacked only 14 times in 16 regular-season games, and it was the first time he was sacked in the playoffs. He set some Super Bowl records—most pass attempts, 50, and most pass completions, 29.

Joe Montana also set a few Super Bowl records, with the most yards passing, 331; the most yards rushing by a quarterback, 59; and the most pass attempts without an interception, 35. He also directed the most productive offense. The 49ers piled up 537 net yards. That is the most impressive record of all.

Joe won the MVP award for the second time. That put him in pretty good company. Only Bart Starr and Terry Bradshaw had won the MVP award twice. And Joe has a pretty good chance of winning that award again soon.

After the Super Bowl, Joe Montana was very patient, as he stayed in the locker room until every reporter's question was answered. He was respectful toward the Dolphins. He tried not to rub it in. But it was hard not to enjoy a game like this. "All we heard all week long was Miami's offense and how are we going to stop them," Joe said. "Nothing was said, but we knew we had an offense, too. No one was thinking about how to stop us."

When the subject turned to his opponent, Joe was generous in his praise. "I knew Marino was better, coming in, based on what he'd done this season," he said. "He's a great quarterback. Having this kind of game is rough, especially in a game like this. He must be a great quarterback or he wouldn't have had the season he did. As far as my own game, well,"—Joe decided not to be humble, just to be honest—"I'd have to admit it was pretty close to the best game I've ever played."

Dan Marino was tight-lipped after the game. His eyes threw daggers at photographers as he unwrapped tape from the knee braces on his legs and from the rest of his bruised, battered body. He removed a protective jacket from his ribs. Then he took a shower. The reporters wondered if he could lose a game as graciously as he'd won so many all year.

Danny was led to the post-game press conference podium and fielded questions from the media. He didn't offer any excuses. Instead, he showed a lot of class and took most of the blame. "In some cases I didn't make good throws," he said. "I didn't play as well as I should have. It's necessary for a quarterback, and it's what Montana did so well today."

After 20 minutes or so, Danny figured he'd said all there was to say. He left the podium, went back to his locker, removed an elegant black suit, and put it on. The TV people turned off their lights.

He turned to a reporter from Miami. "I've handled it before," he said. "You can't dwell on it. It's part of the game. It's something you don't forget about, but you have to take the good with the bad, right?"

He almost managed a smile as he left the locker room. Maybe he was already starting to think about a rematch in Super Bowl XX!

11
Who's the Best?

Before the Super Bowl, or any big football game, comparisons between each team's quarterback are drawn up in the newspapers, and writers pick one over the other. Before Super Bowl XIX, Dan Marino usually got the nod over Joe Montana. If you examine what Danny did in 1984, that almost makes sense. But these two guys are so great, and have such different styles, it's almost impossible to pick one over the other.

First, let's examine their styles. Marino's strongest suit, the one thing everyone marvels at, is his quick release. Joe Namath, who had the quickest release of his time, took 2.2 to 2.7 seconds to get rid of the ball. Marino has been clocked at 1.5 seconds. That's part of the reason he rarely gets sacked. Even if a defensive lineman can get past Miami's offensive line, Danny can dump off a pass before the defender gets within five feet of sacking him.

Another weapon in the Marino Corps arsenal is the quick strike. The classic way of slowing down a passing machine like Dapper Dan is ball control. The logic is that if you keep the ball for long periods of time and use up the clock, you give an explosive offense like Miami's less time to score. It doesn't work with Mr. Marino. The Steelers learned this in the AFC championship game, when Marino blew open what was a close game by scoring touchdowns on three straight possessions. The first touchdown was scored in one minute, 20 seconds. The next touchdown took all of 33 seconds. The third touchdown took a minute and 48 seconds. No sense in eating up the clock against someone who can burn you for 21 points in four minutes.

Marino's flaw is his slow feet. If he's pressured by a great pass rush, as he was in Super Bowl XIX, he doesn't move fast enough. He can make mistakes, although his quick release often covers up this weakness. So does his toughness and his cool under fire. No matter what's thrown against him, he'll stand in there and take it, and do what he has to to get his team moving.

Another advantage Marino has is his exceptionally strong arm. In the Marks Brothers—Duper and Clayton—Danny has two receivers who like to run deep pass patterns, which complements Danny's style. He likes to throw deep. This means that opposing defenses have to open up their secondary, play them deep. That opens up more room to throw short passes. It's tough trying to stop them.

Joe Montana is a different style of quarterback. Although he is capable of throwing the ball deep and keeps defenses honest with an occasional long bomb, he's more comfortable with the short pass. He's got quick, nimble feet that enable him to scramble away from trouble, and his instinctive, analytical mind tells him where his receivers are. So he'll dink and dunk you to death, hitting his pass receivers with short passes while he's rolling out to avoid defensive pressure.

The play that made Montana famous was the swing right option against Dallas in the NFC championship game in the 1981 season. There were 58 seconds left in the game, and the 49ers were six yards away from their first Super Bowl. It was third down, and the Niners used up their second timeout to talk things over. If they couldn't do it here, they had only one chance left. Montana rolled out to the right, spreading out the pass rush. His primary receiver was covered. Joe ran toward the sideline and cocked his arm. He was about to throw the ball away when he saw Dwight Clark open in the end zone and threw it over a bunch of defenders. He almost threw it over Clark, but Dwight somehow jumped up and caught it.

It was a play that only Joe Montana could have pulled off. Montana specializes in stuff only he can do, like scrambling on a busted play and running into the end zone when the defense is so busy covering his receivers that they forget him.

Montana admits that Marino is bigger, stronger, and has a better arm than he does. But Montana does a lot more to beat you than just throw the ball. Like the man says, "it's not the size of the ship that gets you there, it's the motion of the ocean."

A mediocre quarterback, it's sometimes argued, can do exceptionally well under the right system. And a great quarterback can be ruined under the wrong system. Both Montana and Marino were lucky in this regard.

There's no doubt that both quarterbacks fell into ideal situations. Bill Walsh is the ideal coach for Joe Montana. And Montana was just what the doctor ordered for the San Francisco 49ers—a quarterback from a college with the greatest winning tradition on the planet, who could walk in, take over, and lead them.

Dan Marino found what he needed in Miami. Don Shula's discipline, fueled by his own gnawing desire to prove himself to all the teams that passed on him in the college draft, molded him into an awesome offensive force. And it's no coincidence that Mark Duper was discovered in the first game Dan Marino started for the Dolphins. He found the perfect targets, and the rest is history.

Before we go out on a limb and pick out the best quarterback, there are a few rules we'd like to throw at you that we've used.

"One monkey doesn't make a circus." That is, no player in a team sport can be great all by himself. This is especially true in football. Would Dan Marino have thrown 48 TD passes if he didn't have people who could catch the ball? People like Mark Duper, Mark Clayton, and Nat Moore! Would Joe Montana have been the MVP of the Super Bowl if the San Francisco defense allowed the Dolphins to score 100 points? Probably not, right? So we've tried to judge the individuals here, not the teams.

Like they say in Hollywood, "you're only as good as your last movie." More people watch the Super Bowl than any other television event. In fact, for millions of TV viewers, it's the only football game they bother to watch all year. Even after Marino had the season of a lifetime, he ended up the second banana to Joe Montana to most of the public.

The third rule is that, in sports, "it's not what you do, it's how long you do it." Jim Brown may have been the greatest running back of all time, but Walter Payton is in the record books as the all-time best.

Then there's "potential." If you consider what Dan Marino is capable of doing, based on what he's already accomplished, the numbers are mind-boggling. He'll do to the football record book what Wayne Gretzky has done to the hockey record book. He'll own it!

Chuck Noll said, when asked if Danny Marino is the greatest quarterback of all time, "Give him time." Who knows? In five years, the Kid might have five Super Bowl rings. The only thing certain about Dan Marino right now is that, in 1984, he put together the greatest year of any quarterback in NFL history.

Joe Montana has been on top of the mountain long enough to be crowned king. He became pro football's leading passer of all time in November 1983, when his attempts number passed 1500. His rating is 90.7 and still climbing.

Even if Dan Marino continues to perform as well as he has, and passes Montana to become the top-rated QB of all time, he might not be considered the top quarterback until he wins a Super Bowl.

Danny White was the Cowboys' number-one quarterback for years, and was the NFL's top-rated passer before Montana overtook him. Danny White passed Roger Staubach, who was the last Cowboy quarterback to win a Super Bowl. Danny White helped to get the Dallas Cowboys into the NFC title game three years in a row, but couldn't get them into a Super Bowl. Fans, and even teammates, accused

White of being unable to win the big games. So, even though he was the NFL's top-rated passer, he became the Cowboys' number-two quarterback.

Terry Bradshaw, former quarterback of the Pittsburgh Steelers, has said, "He [Marino] is the best I've ever seen." He should know what he's talking about—Bradshaw led the Steelers to four Super Bowl appearances, and won every time.

That's the final test of who's the best—the ring. Bradshaw has four. That's why right now Montana is a better quarterback than Marino. He has two rings. Marino hasn't gotten his yet.

But our prediction is that Marino will get his. And he'll overtake Montana to become the top-rated passer of all time. He'll have a few seasons that surpass what he did in 1984, and he will win a few Super Bowls. After all, he's done everything at an age that saw every great quarterback before him sitting on the bench, trying to adjust to the NFL.

Until he does, Joe Montana is the top quarterback in football. And Dan Marino knows it.

But for our money, picking the best is just about impossible. Their styles, personalities, and situations are so different. So here's the bottom line. Who's the best?

Joe Montana—and Dan Marino.

STATISTICS

JOE MONTANA #16
6′ 2″ 195 lbs., born June 11, 1956
graduated from Notre Dame University

1984 Quarterback Rating

Completions	Attempts	%	Total Yards
279	432	.640	3,630

Average Gain	TDs	TD%	INT	INT%	Rating
8.40	28	6.5	10	2.3	103.0

NFL Regular Season Passing Statistics

Year	Att.	Comp.	Yards	Avg.	TD
1979	23	13	96	4.2	1
1980	273	176	1795	6.6	15
1981	488	311	3565	7.3	19
1982	346	213	2613	7.6	17
1983	515	332	3910	7.6	26
1984	432	327	3630	8.4	28
Totals	2077	1324	15609	6.1	106

DAN MARINO #13
6′ 3″ 214 lbs., born September 15, 1961
graduated from University of Pittsburgh

1984 Quarterback Rating

Completions	Attempts	%	Total Yards		
362	564	.642	5,084		

Average Gain	TDs	TD%	INT	INT%	Rating
9.0	48	8.5	17	3.0	108.9

NFL Regular Season Passing Statistics

Year	Att.	Comp.	Yards	Avg.	TD
1983	296	175	2210	7.4	20
1984	564	362	5084	9.0	48
Totals	860	537	7294	8.2	68

**Other Books in the
Avon Superstar Series:**

Doug Flutie—$2.50